WARNING!

DO NOT OPEN THIS BOOK ABOUT CREDIT

THERE MAY BE SHOCKING INFORMATION INSIDE

WARNING WARNING WARNING WARNING WARNING WARNING WARNING

DOMINICK BURKE

WARNING!
DO NOT OPEN
THIS BOOK
ABOUT CREDIT

ISBN: 978-0-9894680-7-7

Published by:
Divine Works Publishing
Royal Palm Beach, Florida USA
www.divineworkspublishing.com
561-990-BOOK (2665)

ACKNOWLEDGMENTS

First and foremost, all Glory to God for through him all dreams, no matter how big or small, are possible.

To the mentors that have shaped, inspired, and motivated me in the many aspects of my life:

Marie Garvin (my mom whom I love dearly),
Michael Burke,
Bernadette Burke,
Lenore Stewart (my aunt),
Deborah Keys (RCPO),
the late Honorable Harry Edelstein,
Esq., S. Hubert Humphrey,
Toni Lester (nee Arcaro),
Victor Sohm,
B.J.P. Ladson,
Monte Holm,
Lance Vennard,
Joel Pate,
Mike Citron
and John Ulzheimer.

DEDICATIONS

To my children; Naadira, Shakorah and Adrian who are the center of all of my ambitions.

Dedicated to the memory of Fred Burke, Sr, Fred Burke, Jr, Annie Burke (nee Saunders), Phyllis Burke, Thomas Winfrey, Dorothy Eli (nee Stewart), Emma Jean Hester (my beloved Aunt), Kim Hogan, Malcolm Garvin, Lorraine Stokley, Maurice Stokley, Adrian Branch (whom my son was named after), Gertrude (nee Saunders), Dorothy Jones (nee Saunders), Constance Lewis (nee Saunders), Bradley Lewis, Rashee Fa and Joel Pate.

Also dedicated to ALL consumers that have a burning desire to pursue any financial lifestyle upgrades.

And to the woman that has endured the most...Melanie Herman. Thanks for your patience and I love you dearly!

TABLE OF CONTENTS

TABLE X: EIGHT SECRET SCORES

TABLE Y: THE 56 DIFFERENT CREDIT SCORES

CHAPTER 1

WHY DO WE NEED CREDIT AND "GOOD CREDIT?"

"I don't want any credit cards. I don't use credit cards, because I'm one of those people that believe if I don't have the money to purchase something in cash, then I don't need to buy it!" Does this sound at all familiar? Are you one of these people, or do you know someone with this mentality?

Let me be the first to tell you that credit affects many aspects of your life, starting with employment opportunities. How many times have you been rejected for employment? Did you know that every time you apply for a job or a professional license, you authorize a potential employer or licensing authority to order a background/investigative consumer report on you?

Have you ever seen the following Disclosure, Authorization, and Consent on a job application?

DISCLOSURE, AUTHORIZATION, AND CONSENT: As a matter of policy, background check reports are obtained on prospective employees. This policy is a business necessity that protects everyone by helping to promote safe and profitable workplace. All inquiries are limited to information that affects job performance and the workplace. It is conducted in accordance with applicable federal and state laws including the Fair Credit Reporting Act (FCRA). All or a portion of the screening may be conducted by an outside agency retained by our company. Any such background check may contain information bearing on character, general reputation, personal characteristics, mode of living and credit standing. The types of information that may be obtained include, but are not limited to: credit reports, social security number verification, criminal records, public court records, driving records, educational records, verification of employment positions held, workers' compensation records, personal and professional reference checks, licensing and certification checks, etc. The information contained in these check reports may be obtained from private and/or public record sources, including sources identified in this and other job applications or through interviews or correspondence with past or present coworkers, neighbors, friends, associates, current or former employers or educational institutions.Under the Fair Credit Reporting Act, should our company rely upon a credit report for any adverse action, before taking that action you will be provided with a copy of the credit report and a summary of your rights. You will have the right, upon request, to be informed of whether or not a credit report was requested. If a credit report is requested, you will be provided with the name and address of the consumer reporting agency furnishing the report. You may inspect and receive a copy of the report by contacting that agency.By my signature below, I expressly authorize this company and any outside agency retained by this company to perform and release to this company a background check report(s) on me in conjunction with my employment application or my job. I understand that if I am employed by this company, my consent will apply throughout my employment to the extent permitted by law unless I revoke or cancel my consent by sending a signed letter or statement to this company. I understand that, to the extent allowed by law, information contained in my job application or otherwise disclosed by me before, during or after my employment, may be utilized for the purpose of obtaining background check reports.

_____Applicant Signature/Date

Within the language of the above Disclosure, Authorization and Consent, the words 'character' and 'personal characteristics' may justify the pulling of a consumer/credit report in order to measure one's level of accountability and responsibility for employment.

Although we, as credit professionals, cannot determine how an employer or licensing authority may measure or define this for their own policies, we do recognize however, that there may be a direct link between how responsible a consumer is in paying their own bills and how responsible that same consumer behaves in the workplace.

Other information found on your credit report that may be pertinent may be the names of previous employers. We also know that one of the reasons why an employer pulls credit before hiring is they want to know what the chances are that they will have to facilitate a garnishment for a potential employee's creditors. They don't like to spend more money on labor costs every time they have to pay you. Keep in mind that a potential employer can rely on your credit report to make a hiring decision. If it relies upon a credit report for any adverse action, before it takes that action

> "**Contrary to popular opinion, it is cheaper to buy a home than to rent one in 98 out of 100 of the largest metropolitan areas in the United States.**"

you must be provided with a notice that adverse action was taken based on information obtained from a consumer reporting agency and a summary of your rights under the Fair Credit Reporting Act (FCRA).

We have found many instances where potential employers have violated the FCRA by not informing applicants that they were not hired based on information provided through their credit reports. Another aspect of your life that credit has a critical effect upon is residency. Whether you seek to rent or own a home, credit inquiries will be made into your previous payment history.

Is it cheaper to rent or own property? Contrary to popular opinion, it is cheaper to buy a home than to rent one in 98 out of 100 of the largest metropolitan areas in the United States. What makes this possible? A surplus of homes cannot be sold by real estate investors to earn a profit because mortgage balances exceed market values. Investors are in over their heads. Investors must pay mortgage payments, property, and school taxes. Many investors own multiple properties. Investors are constantly looking for renters to minimize or eliminate their monthly liabilities. To meet these liabilities, rent payments can be high. To reiterate, it is cheaper to own but there are obstacles that stand in the way of ownership. Credit is one of the primary obstacles. The standard for credit-worthiness is different for a 30-year mortgage than it is for a 1-year lease. The second obstacle is income. There are many properties you can rent without having to provide proof of income. With such abundance of foreclosed properties over the last decade, approval for a mortgage is almost impossible without overlapping evidence of income.

Whether you rent or own, utilities such as gas and electric are needed for the home. Have you ever heard of the National Consumer Telecom & Utilities Exchange (NCTUE)? It is a member-owned database housed and managed by Equifax Information Services. Membership is available to the nation's leading Telecommunication, Pay TV and Utility companies. NCTUE exchanges information on new connects and defaulted and/or fraudulent accounts among members. It provides access to current contact information on defaulted consumers and customized treatment and collection strategies for new applicants and existing customers who have unpaid bills.

In layman's terms, there is now a consumer reporting agency (much like the major credit bureaus) that houses information on anyone who has had a mobile phone or utility bill. When you call the electric company to turn on your electricity, this is the company that will more than likely provide information that will make it easier to gauge your default risk for failure to pay late or not pay at all.

Ultimate denial of utility service may sit with this company alone. It is important for consumers to know that there are well over 40 different consumer reporting agencies that store payment-related information from every single aspect of your life as a consumer.

> ⚠ **WARNING:**
> Pay ALL bills on time; not just credit accounts!

CHAPTER 2

UNDERSTANDING YOUR CREDIT REPORT

There are usually six sections to a credit report: Personal Information, Summary, Account History, Public Record Information, Inquiries, and Creditor Contacts.

Let's discuss them one section at a time.

SAMPLE CREDIT REPORT
Ben Hollering
September 6, 2012

Personal Information

	Experian	TransUnion	Equifax
Name:	Ben Hollering	Ben R. Hollering	Ben Hollering
Year of Birth:	1971	1971	1971
Address(es):	456 Broadway	456 Broadway Apt 2	456 Broadway Apt 2
	New York, NY 10003	New York, NY 10003	New York, NY 10003
	321 Montague St	2468 Columbus Circle	
	Brooklyn, NY 11203	New York, NY 10018	

Previous Employer: US Postal Service
Current Employer: NYC MTA

As you can see above, the **Personal Information** section contains information about your name, addresses and employment.

Summary

Real Estate Accts	Experian	TransUnion	Equifax
Count:	1	1	1
Balance ($):	194973	194973	194973
Payment ($):	1129	1129	1129
Current:	1	1	1
Delinquent:	0	0	0
Derogatory:	0	0	0
Revolving Accts	**Experian**	**TransUnion**	**Equifax**
Count:	4	3	5
Balance ($):	2271	906	1118
Payment ($):	1118	906	1125
Current:	1	1	1
Delinquent:	0	0	0
Derogatory:	0	0	0

The **Summary** section contains a list of payment history, broken down by account type and count. The summary section includes a categorized list of all the accounts on the credit report. This overview allows you to quickly review the credit profile and compare data among the 3 main credit bureaus.

The five types of accounts listed in the Summary section (three are not listed in the above example) include the following:

- **Real Estate:** Primary and secondary real estate mortgages.
- **Revolving:** Accounts comprised of open terms with varying payments (e.g. credit card account)
- **Installment:** Accounts comprised of fixed terms with regular payments (e.g. auto loan)
- **Other:** Accounts in which the exact category is unknown. This could include 30-day open accounts such as an American Express account. You may hear some people refer to these types of accounts as charge cards.
- **Collection:** Accounts seriously past due include accounts assigned to an attorney, collection agency or creditor's in-house collection department.

The **Summary** section also includes the following information for each of the five types of accounts:

- **Count:** Total number of accounts in the given category.
- **Balance:** Total amount owed on all accounts in that specific category.
- **Payment:** Total monthly payments required on all accounts in that specific category.
- **Current:** Number of accounts in the category that are properly paid.
- **Delinquent:** Number of accounts in the category for which payments are past due
- **Derogatory:** Number of accounts that have a negative impact on credit rating.
- **Unknown:** Number of accounts in the category whose condition was not reported by the credit bureau. The Unknown sub-category section also summarizes the customer's open accounts, closed accounts, public records and inquires which are further explained below:

Open/Closed Accounts: A total number of all accounts that are either open or closed.

Public Records: A count of any public records in the consumer's name and the total amount of money involved for all public records. Public records may include judgments in civil actions, state or federal tax liens and bankruptcies.

Inquiries: An inquiry appears when an organization such as a bank or retail store requests a copy of a credit report within the last two years.

Account History

Creditor Name	Experian	TransUnion	Equifax
Account Number:	1234xxxx	1234xxxx	123456xx
Type:	Real Estate	RE Mortgage	Real Estate Mortgage
Responsibility:	Individual	Individual	Individual
Pay Status:	60 days late	Charge-off	30 days late
Date Opened:	02/02/2000	02/2000	02/2000
Date Reported:	08/01/2000	08/01/2000	08/01/2000
Balance and Limit:	$112755	$112755	$112755
Payment/Terms:	$1129 for 36 mths	$1129 for 36 mths	$1129 for 36 mths
High Balance:	$113679	$113679	$113679
Past Due:	$0	$0	$0
Remarks:			

Two Year Payment History:

Experian

Sep	Oct	Nov	Dec	Jan	Feb	Mar	Apr	May	Jun	Jul	Aug	Sep	Oct	Dec	Jan	Feb	Mar	Apr	May	Jun	Jul	Aug	Sep
																				30	60		

TransUnion

Sep	Oct	Nov	Dec	Jan	Feb	Mar	Apr	May	Jun	Jul	Aug	Sep	Oct	Dec	Jan	Feb	Mar	Apr	May	Jun	Jul	Aug	Sep
																				30	60	CO	

Equifax

Sep	Oct	Nov	Dec	Jan	Feb	Mar	Apr	May	Jun	Jul	Aug	Sep	Oct	Dec	Jan	Feb	Mar	Apr	May	Jun	Jul	Aug	Sep
																				30			

The **Account History** section provides detailed information about all credit accounts. Accounts are divided into five categories: Real Estate, Revolving, Installment, Other and Collections.

- **Creditor Name:** The abbreviated name of the person or agency that provided the credit account, such as a bank, credit card company or mortgage lender
- **Account Number:** An identifying number for the account. Typically, this would be a credit card number for a credit card account or a loan identification number for a mortgage.
- **Type:** The type of account. Some common account types are Real Estate, Automobile, Educational (Student Loans) and Credit Card or Revolving.
- **Condition:** A detailed description of the account's payment status as of the last reporting date.
- **Responsibility:** The role in the account. For example, "Individual" or "Joint."

• **Pay Status:** The state of the account. For example, "Open" or "Closed."
 • **Date Opened:** The date when the account was opened
 • **Date Reported**: The last date any activity in this account was shown. Activities include payments, credit card billings, etc.
 • **Balance and Limit:** The amount presently owed on the account (based on the last reported activity) compared to the maximum amount of credit approved.
 • **Payment and Terms:** The amount and number of monthly payments scheduled.
 • **High Balance:** The most ever owed on this account. In the case of a credit card, for example, this would be the highest balance ever accumulated. For a mortgage, it would be the initial amount of the mortgage, not the current paid-down principal.
 • **Past Due:** The amount of payment overdue as of the most recently reported activity.
 • **Remarks:** If there are any remarks about the account.
 • **Two Year Payment History:** At the bottom of the account information, there is a month-to-month payment history for the previous 24 months.

The abbreviations in this section equate to the following:
30 = 30 days late,
60 = 60 days late,
90 = 90 days late,
120 = 120 days late
CO = Account is in Collections
 K or KD = Key Derogatory (e.g. Late Payment)
 X = Unknown, which could mean the credit bureaus have not received any information from the creditors to report that month.

Public Record Information

Bankruptcy	Experian	TransUnion	Equifax
Type:	Chapter 7	Chapter 7	Chapter 7
Status:	Filed	Filed	Filed
Date filed/Reported:	09/2010	09/2010	09/2010
How filed:	Individual	Individual	Individual
Reference #:	MI3-7844	MI3-7844	MI3-7844
Closing Date:	03/2011	04/2011	03/2011
Court:	Cobb County	Cobb County	Cobb Cnty
Amount:	$11,798	$11,798	$11,798
Remarks:			

The **Public Record Information** section lists publicly available information about legal matters affecting credit. These public records may include judgments in civil actions, state or federal tax liens and bankruptcies.

Inquiries

Creditor Name	Experian	TransUnion	Equifax
Bank A	08/2012		08/2012
Credit Card Co A	01/2012	01/2012	
Credit Card Co B	09/2011	09/2011	09/2011
Mortgage Lender		08/2011	
Department Store		05/2011	05/2011

The *Inquiries* section lists details about each inquiry that has been made into one's credit history. Details include the name of the creditor or potential creditor who made the inquiry and the date on which the inquiry was made. These requests can only be made if the customer has a credit granting relationship or is applying for credit with the organization. The requester's (creditor) name will appear on the credit report, allowing the customer to monitor who accessed the credit report.

Creditor Contacts

Creditor Name	Address	Phone Number
Bank A	142 Davidson Street, Anytown, NY 12468	(888) 000-1234
Credit Card Co A	122-08 Irwin Place, Funville, NV 89100	(800) 111-7890

⚠ WARNING:
Anything in RED in the Account History section has a negative effect on credit scores!

CHAPTER 3

WHO AND WHAT CREATES YOUR CREDIT SCORE?

C redit scores are created by FICO (Fair Isaac Corporation), isn't that right? WRONG! FICO creates software that it sells and licenses to the credit bureaus.

Each credit bureau has its own proprietary version of FICO Software. The software allows the credit bureaus to input credit history information that it stores on millions of consumers that have had any loans or lines of credit. Credit bureaus are only in the business of storing information that is reported to them by creditors.

Creditors usually furnish the credit bureaus with monthly updates regarding the consumer's account(s). To provide some visual frame of reference, please view the following: FICO creates a calculator with

a formula that contains unknown variables such as:
$A2 + B7 \times C12 - D9 \div E4 = $ Credit Score

A Credit Bureau would then purchase the calculator (software) with the formula from FICO and will input consumer credit information that it has on file to replace the A, B, C, D and E in the above formula to arrive at a Credit Score.

A = Number of Late Payments
B = Outstanding Balances
C = Length of Credit History
D = How Many Different Types of Credit
E = Number of Credit Inquiries (last 12 months)

Generally, credit scores are 3-digit numbers ranging from 300 – 850, which are used to predict the likelihood a person will pay back or default on a loan or line of credit.

A credit score is calculated based on information from the following key areas:

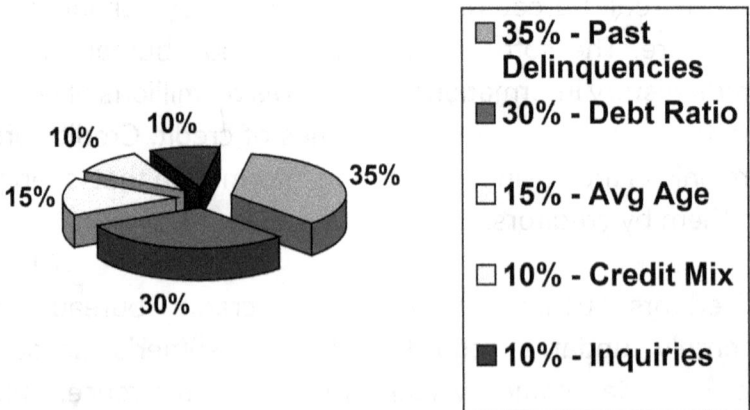

10% 10%
15%
35%
30%

- 35% - Past Delinquencies
- 30% - Debt Ratio
- 15% - Avg Age
- 10% - Credit Mix
- 10% - Inquiries

Past delinquencies would include such things as late payments or non-payments and **accounts for 35% of the credit score.**

Debt ratio is determined by dividing your total balances by your total lines of credit. **This accounts for 30% of the credit score.**

The average age of each account is determined by adding all the years each account has been in existence and dividing those total years by the total number of accounts on a credit report. **The average age accounts for 15% of the credit score.**

Credit mix is simply a mixture of revolving credit and installment loans and **this accounts for 10% of the credit score.**

An inquiry into your credit takes place when you apply for a loan or line of credit. **The number of inquiries into one's credit within a certain window of time accounts for 10% of the credit score.**

> ### ⚠ WARNING:
> Be selective about applying for credit lines. Resist the urge to be impulsive. These days everyone is offering credit lines.
> Be selective!

CHAPTER 4

WHO ARE THE BIG 3?

C redit bureaus are consumer reporting agencies. A consumer reporting agency is any company that collects and stores information about a consumer's borrowing and/or payment habits. It sells that information via credit reports to lenders, landlords, employers, credit card companies, insurance companies and licensing agencies.

Most lenders order credit reports from three major credit bureaus. They are Experian, Equifax, and TransUnion and these are known as the "Big 3".

These three major credit bureaus are utilized to provide a Tri-Merge (3-bureau) credit report. A Tri-Merge report provides a side-by-side comparison of information reported to all three major credit bureaus. However, there is a fourth and a fifth major credit bureau. They are Innovis and PRBC. Innovis sells consumer information to companies that would like to solicit you for their products or services through pre-approval offers. PRBC is an abbreviation for Pay Rent, Build Credit, Inc. It differs from the other four credit bureaus. It allows consumers to self-enroll to report their own non-debt payment history such as rent, utilities, cable, telephone and insurance payments.

Experian, Equifax and Transunion are all publicly-traded companies that generate a combined revenue of $9.4 Billion with Experian leading the pack in (2016). One of the biggest misconceptions about the Credit Bureaus is that they are agencies of the U.S. Government and they are NOT! Another big misconception is that lenders and creditors are required to report payment information and they are NOT! However, if they choose to report information regarding your accounts or payment history, they are required to report accurate, complete, and verifiable information under the Fair Credit Reporting Act (FCRA).

> **Over the last 20 years, I personally have reviewed well over 10,000 credit reports, and about one out of every four reports I reviewed, had consumer-alleged errors...**

Other notable consumer reporting agencies include ChexSystems, Inc. and CoreLogic SafeRent. ChexSystems, Inc. provides data related to consumer banking activities and irregularities such as check overdrafts, unsatisfied balances, deposited fraudulent checks or other suspicious activities. This is a company that can make it difficult for you to open a new bank account. CoreLogic SafeRent collects and reports comprehensive information about landlord-tenant actions (such as prior evictions), address history, public background check (to identify prior criminal and court judgments, including prior prison sentences, presence on government-managed sex offender and known terrorist databases).

Although consumer reporting agencies/credit bureaus house information on millions of consumers, it was proven by the U.S. Public Interest Research Group back in 2004 that 79% of the credit reports surveyed contained either serious errors or other mistakes.

With all of the technology and laws in place, how does this happen? Who is to blame? Over the last 20 years, I personally have reviewed well over 10,000 credit reports and it seemed to me that one out of every four reports that I reviewed, had consumer-alleged errors that were corrected after I initiated dispute investigations and I've found both the reporting agencies and creditors were to blame for inaccurate and outdated information.

> ### ⚠ WARNING:
> Undisputed inaccurate information can adversely affect your credit score!

CHAPTER 5

COMMON AND CRITICAL ERRORS ON CREDIT REPORTS

Sometimes the consumer reporting agencies/credit bureaus are responsible for errors on a credit report and other times the creditors are responsible. The average consumer may experience many challenges in conducting their own investigation when trying to figure out who is to blame for such damaging errors. It may be wise to seek the services of a credit expert to investigate who is to blame.

Many consumers experience wrong information on their credit reports such as:

- Accounts that aren't theirs. Sometimes there are 'mis-merges' that people with similar names such as "John Doe" are confused with John A. Doe."
- An account that says it was closed by (credit) grantor when in fact the consumer voluntarily canceled one of their credit cards.

- Accounts that had been closed by the consumer but incorrectly listed as open.
- Debts that have been discharged in bankruptcy and bad debts that are at least seven (7)years old. The reporting of discharged debts is a very common error.
- The wrong date the account was opened.
- The wrong balance amount
- Inaccurate late payment information
- Inaccurate 'past due' amount
- Inaccurate 'high balance' amount
- Inaccurate account statuses (e.g. Collections, Charge-off, etc.)
- Inaccurate account types (e.g. Revolving, Installment or Other)
- Inaccurate account ownership (e.g. Individual or Joint)
- Inaccurate personal information (e.g. name, address, employer names, etc.)

Then there are people such as Kathleen Casey, Gina Marie Haynes, and Dennis Teague, all of who have had to deal with severe consequences as a result of inaccurate reporting and information on their consumer reports.

Kathleen Casey, like many other Americans had experienced unemployment for a few years and her unemployment benefits had expired. She did land an $11 an hour job at a pharmacy in Boston under the condition that she would pass a background check. The background check fetched a 14-count criminal indictment involving a larceny charge in a scam against an elderly man and woman that involved forged checks and fake credit cards. But guess what? This was a huge mistake on the part of First Advantage, the consumer reporting agency used to run the background check. The rap

COMMON AND CRITICAL ERRORS ON CREDIT REPORTS

sheet belonged to a woman with a similar name, Kathleen A. Casey, who lived in a nearby town and was 18 years younger. Needless to say, Kathleen Casey did not get the job. One of the biggest misconceptions about credit reporting is that ALL information populates onto a credit file based ONLY on the Social Security Number. As in the case of Kathleen Casey, oftentimes it does not.

Gina Marie Haynes had relocated to Philadelphia from Texas in the summer of 2010 and had a similar experience. She landed a job managing apartments pending the outcome of a background check. To her disappointment, the background check uncovered fraud charges. After purchasing a Saab, and driving it off the lot, the engine started smoking. The dealer charged her close to $300 for repairs. After she refused to pay for the repairs, the dealer filed fraud charges. After six months, she gave up her protest of the charges and paid the bill. If anyone had looked at her paper file at her local courthouse, they would have seen that the fraud charge had been removed prior to the background check. The problem was that the consumer reporting agency reported 'outdated' data on her background check.

> "All consumer reporting agencies must conform to the Fair Credit Reporting Act (FCRA) by providing accurate, verifiable and updated information on consumers."

Dennis Teague was a victim of inaccurate information as well. He was rejected for a job in Wisconsin because of a background check that showed a 13-page rap sheet listing gun and drug crimes along with long periods of incarceration. Needless to say, it wasn't an accurate depiction of his character.

Instead, his cousin had committed criminal impersonation by giving Dennis' name during an arrest.

All consumer reporting agencies must conform to the Fair Credit Reporting Act (FCRA) by providing accurate, verifiable and updated information on consumers.

Although there are no preemptive measures that a consumer can take to prevent the reporting of inaccurate, unverifiable and outdated information, the FCRA and other Federal and State Laws provide relief for damages and injuries. There were 3,960 lawsuits filed in 2016 for violations of the FCRA.

⚠ WARNING:
Seek the help of a credit repair expert if you are experiencing errors on your credit report and are not sure where to start.

CHAPTER 6

IS CREDIT REPAIR LEGAL?

Many consumers and companies think that credit repair is illegal. Let me be the first to tell you that Credit Repair is 100% LEGAL!

If credit repair was deemed illegal, the U.S. Government would not regulate the activities of credit repair organizations through 15 U.S.C. § 1679 otherwise known as the Credit Repair Organizations Act ("CROA") which we have provided for your review toward the end of this book. This act regulates the activities of Credit Repair Organizations that provide credit repair services for consumers. Within the scope of CROA, there is language that requires credit repair organizations to provide a consumer with the following notice:

You have a right to dispute inaccurate information in your credit report by contacting the credit bureau directly. However, neither you nor any "credit repair" company or credit repair organization has the right to have accurate, current, and verifiable information removed from your credit report. The credit bureau must remove accurate, negative information from your report only if it is over 7 years old. Bankruptcy information can be reported for 10 years.

You have a right to obtain a copy of your credit report from a credit bureau. You may be charged a reasonable fee. There is no fee, however, if you have been turned down for credit, employment, insurance, or a rental dwelling because of information in your credit report within the preceding 60 days. The credit bureau must provide someone to help you interpret the information in your credit file. You are entitled to receive a free copy of your credit report if you are unemployed and intend to apply for employment in the next 60 days, if you are a recipient of public welfare assistance, or if you have reason to believe that there is inaccurate information in your credit report due to fraud.

You have a right to sue a credit repair organization that violates the Credit Repair Organization Act. This law prohibits deceptive practices by credit repair organizations.

You have the right to cancel your contract with any credit repair organization for any reason within 3 business days from the date you signed it.

Credit bureaus are required to follow reasonable procedures to ensure that the information they report is accurate. However, mistakes may occur.

You may, on your own, notify a credit bureau in writing that you dispute the accuracy of information in your credit file. The credit bureau must then reinvestigate and modify or remove inaccurate or incomplete information. The credit bureau may not charge any fee for this service. Any pertinent information and copies of all documents you have concerning an error should be given to the credit bureau.

If the credit bureau's reinvestigation does not resolve the dispute to your satisfaction, you may send a brief statement to the credit bureau, to be kept in your file, explaining why you think the record is inaccurate. The credit bureau must include a summary of your statement about disputed information with any report it issues about you.

The Federal Trade Commission regulates credit bureaus and credit repair organizations. For more information contact:

The Public Reference Branch
Federal Trade Commission
Washington, D.C. 20580'.

One of the purposes of this notice is to inform consumers that they can repair their credit on their own. In my opinion, it can be done but it is a tall order to fill when you have to rummage through the following laws to make sure your rights as a consumer are being enforced by the credit bureaus/consumer reporting agencies, lenders, creditors, employers or insurance companies:

- **RESPA** *(Real Estate Settlement Procedures Act)*
- **FDCPA** *(Fair Debt Collection Practices Act)*
- **FACTA** *(Fair and Accurate Credit Transactions Act)*
- **HIPAA** *(Health Insurance Portability & Accountability Act)*
- **FCRA** *(Fair Credit Reporting Act)*
- **FCBA** *(Fair Credit Billing Act)*
- **TILA** *(Truth-in Lending Act)*
- **GLB** *(Gramm-Leach Bliley Act)*
- **HEA** *(Higher Education Act)*
- **ECOA** *(Equal Credit Opportunity Act)*

An attorney, credit expert, or reputable credit repair organization may be better suited for this type of work than the average consumer. I always wondered why the government advises consumers to repair their own credit when they don't give the same advice for any other service in any other industry. Think about it! They don't tell you that you don't need an Investment Advisor because you can invest your own money. They don't tell you that you can represent yourself in a court of law. They don't tell you that you can cut your own hair, but

> "An attorney, credit expert or reputable credit repair organization may be better suited for this type of work than the average consumer."

if you let the barber cut it and he doesn't comply with the law, you can sue him. They don't tell you that opening a savings account puts your money at risk and can be lost if the bank becomes insolvent. The FDIC insures up to $250,000 per AC-COUNTHOLDER. What this means is that if John Doe has $1,000,000 deposited among 4 different accounts and the bank becomes insolvent, he is at a loss for $750,000. How come consumers are not put on notice for this type of potential risk? I get a sense that there may be some bias against credit repair organizations.

I feel that it is necessary for Credit repair organizations to be regulated through CROA because there have been companies that have been involved with unscrupulous and fraudulent activities. However, equal scrutiny and disclosure should be extended to the consumer for all service-driven industries.

Despite the negative publicity waged against some credit repair organizations, I feel that an attorney, credit expert, or reputable credit repair organization could provide the best chance for a consumer to establish credit or delete inaccurate, unverifiable, outdated information from a credit report. This is because an attorney, credit expert, or credit repair organization may have more experience in navigation and communication with the credit bureaus and creditors than the consumer may have. Simply put, repetition is the mother of all skill!

⚠ WARNING:
Don't blindly attempt to repair your credit.
Credit Repair Organizations can offer valuable assistance and impressive results.

CHAPTER 7

HOW TO ESTABLISH, MAINTAIN, AND IMPROVE CREDIT

If one doesn't have any credit, they are rendered a non-citizen in the world of commerce and finance. You simply do not exist to the banks and it will be difficult to get a loan or line of credit without any experience in borrowing and paying back.

I like to associate consumer credit with 4 stages; a freshman, a sophomore, a junior and a senior.

As a *"freshman"*, a consumer needs to open a bank account and never overdraw that bank account. You will be charged fees and you could damage a good credit reference. Secondly, a freshman needs to open 2 or 3 separate credit accounts. Total purchases should never exceed 30% of the total line of credit on revolving accounts and payments must be paid on time. For example, a consumer that has a $1,000 line of revolving credit should never make purchases that exceed $300. Opening the first account can be difficult but not impossible.

Consumers with no credit history seem to be currently opening accounts with the following entities with relative ease:

- Fingerhut (FreshStart Account): www.fingerhut.com/freshstart
- Hutton Chase: https://www.huttonchase.com/join/?aff=XX-E8D2GP
- Get a Trade Line: http://www.getatradeline.com/?a_aid=73483
- My Jewelers Club: https://www.myjewelersclub.com/discount/26387
- Secured Credit Cards: http://www.creditcardbroker.com/member-detail/?tid=5604
- Credit Builder Card: https://www.creditbuildercard.com/aquarianbusinessgroup.html

I would consider a consumer a **"sophomore"** 6 to 12 months after opening their first set of accounts if they have paid their payments on time and kept their revolving account balances under 30% of the total credit line.

For me to consider a consumer a **"junior"**, they would have to fulfill the sophomore profile above for at least 24 months and have a mixture of different types of accounts.

There are 3 different types of accounts. **They are revolving credit, installment loans, and 'other'.** Revolving credit would be any credit cards, department store cards (e.g. Macy's, Sears, etc.) and gas cards, etc. Installment loans would be auto loans, student loans, CD/Savings secured loans and mortgages. 'Other' is usually a miscellaneous category for such things as charge cards like American Express. Charge cards usually require the balance to be paid in full (PIF) within 30 or 60 days.

For someone to climb the ranks into **"senior"** status, they should have at least 6 different accounts encompassing all 3 different types of accounts for at least 5 years and all revolving account balances must be kept below 30%.

Here are some tips for you to improve your credit:

- *If you haven't made payments on time, start paying on time and stay consistent.*
- *If you have 1 or 2 late payments, ask your creditor for a 'Goodwill deletion'. Sometimes a creditor will delete your late payment info. There is a good chance they will cut you some slack.*
- *If you have accounts that have gone into collection, sometimes collectors will agree to remove the debt from your credit report if you agree to pay it off. Make sure to get this in writing and keep your receipts in a safe place!*
- *If your balances on your revolving accounts exceed 30%, you must bring those balances below 30% and keep them there. Try to focus on keeping your balances in the optimum range of 1% to 5%.*

> **Try to focus on keeping your balances in the optimum range of 1% to 5%.**

- *Ask your significant other, parent or child with good credit to add you as an authorized user or joint account holder on their credit card. It is NOT recommended to be added to someone's account with an opening date that pre-dates your 18th birthday.*

After improving your credit, we have provided the following tips to maintain good credit:

- Review your credit report annually for accuracy. It may be to your benefit to subscribe to a credit monitoring service to receive monthly access to your credit report and monitor alerts for ID Theft.
- Consult with a credit repair expert if you would like to dispute an item on your credit report that is inaccurate, unverifiable or outdated.
- Consult with a credit repair expert prior to consolidating all of your payments into one monthly payment. This usually has a negative impact on your credit scores.
- Consult with a credit repair expert prior to closing any of your credit cards. Closing your credit cards can hurt your score.
- Consult with a credit repair expert prior to applying for credit anywhere. Applying for credit more than once or twice every 12 months could hurt your score.
- Pay all unpaid library fines, parking and speeding tickets. With local municipalities and non-profit entities in a pinch for money, many have contracted with collection agencies to recover debts owed. Needless to say, these debts are reported to the credit bureaus.

⚠ **WARNING:**
Consolidating your debt can have a negative impact on your credit scores!

CHAPTER 8

30 MYTH-CONCEPTIONS ABOUT CREDIT

1. You share a credit score with your spouse.

2. Your credit score only counts when you're looking to borrow money.

3. Always pay your credit card balance in full and that will give you the best credit.

4. My mortgage broker can use the credit report I obtained from www.annualcreditreport.com

5. Too many accounts will hurt, therefore you must close accounts.

6. A co-signer is not responsible

7. If a judge in a divorce proceeding orders spouse 'A' to pay spouse 'B's' debt and spouse 'A' doesn't, it will not affect the credit of spouse 'B'.

8. Piggybacking does not work anymore.

9. Opting out of credit offers will increase your credit score.

10. Multiple auto loan inquiries within a short period of time will hurt your credit score.

11. It will take me seven years to improve my credit.

12. A serious financial crisis like a foreclosure or bankruptcy permanently hurts your credit score.

13. FICO scores are locked in for six months and they change every six months.

14. I don't need to check my credit report if I pay my bills on time.

15. Checking my own credit report harms my credit standing.

16. Consolidating into a low interest-rate credit card will increase your score.

17. Going over the balances on your credit limits are okay because the credit card company authorized the purchase(s).

18. As long as you pay off your credit card balances, your credit score will go up.

19. Types of credit don't matter.

20. Paying off an old collection account or charge-off will increase your credit score.

21. Using debit cards will help you build credit.

22. The credit bureaus are government agencies.

23. If I get one credit bureau to remove an item from my credit report, all the other bureaus will remove it automatically.

24. Credit repair is against the law.

25. Your salary makes a difference in your credit score.

26. Adding a consumer statement to your credit file always improves your credit score.

27. Your credit score alone determines whether or not you get a mortgage.

28. All inquiries into your credit will bring your credit score down.

29. Where I reside affects my credit score.

30. Receiving public assistance affects my credit score.

CHAPTER 9

56 DIFFERENT CREDIT SCORES AVAILABLE THROUGH FICO

Why are all of my credit scores are different? There are two important points that I must make regarding the difference in the numbers. The first thing you need to understand is that all 3 of the major credit bureaus have purchased their own proprietary software from FICO to calculate credit scores. Why proprietary? Because, each bureau has its own way of doing business and has varying information about a consumer when compared to the other 2 credit bureaus.

So the software used to calculate the credit score for any consumer has to be custom-tailored for each of the 3 different business models. This is the reason why most consumers have 3 different credit scores when they apply for a mortgage.

Another thing that consumers need to understand is that creditors are not required to report payment information to all 3 credit bureaus. Oftentimes, some only report to 1 credit bureau. This is also why there is disparity among the credit scores as well.

Putting this point aside, there is something a little more complicated that I need to explain. Not only does FICO create software for each of the credit bureaus. It also creates multiple types of software for each credit bureau to measure different types of consumer risk associated with potential late payment and default patterns. We call these "Scoring Models."

There are scoring models used to specifically measure default risks associated with Auto Loans. FICO has created the following proprietary software for each credit bureau to measure these risks:

- FICO Risk Model V3 Auto (EXPERIAN)
- Beacon 5.0 Auto (EQUIFAX)
- FICO Classic 04 Auto (TRANSUNION)

There are scoring models used to specifically measure default risks associated with Residential Loans (Mortgages). FICO has created the following software for each credit bureau to measure these risks:

- FICO Risk Model V3 Installment Loan (EXPERIAN)
- Beacon 5.0 Mortgage (EQUIFAX)
- FICO Classic 04 Installment Loan (TRANSUNION)

Wouldn't it be fair to measure performance in specific areas that are relevant to the type of credit that a consumer is applying for? In all fairness, a coach who is looking for an athlete to join his/her soccer team should never rely on the athlete's passer rating acquired as a Quarterback in an American Football league. Soccer is a sport based heavily on kicking accuracy. American football is based heavily on passing accuracy. A person's credit score may be higher or lower under different types of credit scoring models because different factors are often used to calculate a credit score.

Here is an educational table that may give you a better understanding of point accumulations under an Application Score for Underwriting approval from a Mortgage Lender using non-credit reporting factors that may not exist in an Auto Loan FICO Scoring model:

Factors		Points
Banking References/Confirmed Activity (Avg monthly and yearly balances) (Age of Accounts)	Checking Savings Multiple Other No activity	5 10 20 11 9
Rent/Own	Own Rent No history	25 15 17
Years at Current Address	Less than 6 months 6 months – 2 yrs 5 mos 2.5 yrs – 6 yrs 5 mos 6.5 yrs – 10 yrs 5 mos 10.5 years +	10 12 15 19 23
Debt-to-Income Ratios (DTI)	Less than 15% 15% - 25% 26% - 35% 36% - 49% 50% +	22 15 12 5 0

Application Scores are 1 of 8 Secret Credit Scores that consumers do not have access to.

FICO has a minimum of 56 different (commercial) scoring models that could potentially produce 56 different scores for each consumer. Do not get upset when you go to a car dealership and get one credit score and then a week later apply for a mortgage and get a completely different score.

To see the 56 Different FICO Scoring Models, please refer to Table X at the end of this book. To see the 8 Secret Scores, please refer to Table Y at the end of this book.

Outside of FICO, other scoring models exist but are rarely relied upon by lenders and creditors. Some of these are VantageScore, PLUS Score and TransRisk Score. These are also called alternative scores. They can be used for educational purposes but in my opinion, they should not be used by the consumer as reliable numbers for loans and other credit decisions.

⚠ WARNING:
Scoring models can reflect a huge disparity
in credit scores depending on the creditor's criteria. This can
work to your advantage once you are clear and consistent with
your financial goals.

CHAPTER 10

THINGS TO BE WARY OF IN THE NEAR FUTURE

In addition to the reporting of derogatory payment information to the credit bureaus, there may be other consequences for inaccurate or negative credit information on your report. Have you ever heard of a DEBTOR'S PRISON?

Back in the 1830's, the U.S. outlawed debtors' prisons, but now it seems like more than a third of the United States allow people to be hauled in for owing all types of debts from medical bills to credit cards and auto loans.

In the spring of 2011, a breast cancer survivor from Herrin, Illinois by the name of Lisa Lindsay did end up behind bars for not paying a medical bill that she was told she didn't owe. She received a $280 medical bill in error and was told she didn't have to pay it. But, the bill was turned over to a collection agency and eventually state troopers showed up at her home and arrested her.

Would you believe it if I told you that Facebook and other Social platforms could hurt your credit rating in the near future? There are several online banks that are currently analyzing your social media profile to determine how big a credit risk you are.

How would they be able to determine that? When you register with a bank to apply for a loan, you would be required to verify your login information for your social network. Information gathered from your accounts would be fed into a formula.

Lenddo (www.lenddo.com) is a company based out of Hong Kong that happens to be the world's first online platform that uses social media to measure creditworthiness. The company takes the wealth of data from your many social networks (including Facebook, LinkedIn, Twitter), looks at the people in your Lenddo Trusted Network (family, friends, co- workers), verifies you have a full-time job, and uses predictive algorithms to confirm your identity and calculate if you are a risk. There are three types of algorithms it uses: Bayesian (pattern matching), validators (verifying your identity and the information you've given), homophily (you're likely to associate with people similar to you). Based on your 'LIKES' on Facebook, they can establish a consumer profile and categorize you with other people with similar characteristics much like FICO can group people together in one peer group with the same borrowing and payment habits. It seems that there is validity to the statement, "Birds of the same feather always flock together."

The following are examples of statements and situations that could disparage OR encourage the credit approval under future credit scoring models:

- If your Facebook friend took out a loan and paid it back, that means you probably will too.
- I just got laid off. Does anyone know who is hiring?
- Sometimes I feel like giving up on life. This might make the bank or an insurance company very uncomfortable.
- Works at ABC Incorporated. If the name of your employer on Facebook differs from the name of the employer you put on a credit application, it might prove that you fabricated information. This may raise eyebrows and may require further investigation for approval OR denial altogether.
- I just got a raise.
- I won a street race with my new Camaro. I won $1,000! Any risky behavior makes you a high risk for loans and insurance.
- I'm now vested with my employer for our 401(k) plan

Another company that collects information through social media sites and other sources is Acxiom (www.acxiom. com). Acxiom collects Facebook "likes", shares, and recommendations. It then analyzes and parses customer and business information for clients to build out a profile of Facebook users to help its clients target advertising campaigns, score leads, and more.

In conclusion, I will leave you with this final note. The Fair Debt Collection Practices Act 15 USC § 1692(b) says that a debt collector is allowed to make one attempt to communicate with any third party ONLY in an attempt to locate you by confirming or correcting location information. Could it be possible for a debt collector to contact any one of your Facebook friends? The answer is YES!

⚠ WARNING:
NEVER POST PRIVATE INFORMATION ON SOCIAL NETWORKING SITES!

APPENDIX A

The Credit Repair Organizations Act "CROA" (15 U.S.C. § 1679)
CHAPTER 2--CREDIT REPAIR ORGANIZATIONS(1)
SEC. 2451. REGULATION OF CREDIT REPAIR ORGANIZATIONS.
Title IV of the Consumer Credit Protection Act (Public Law 90-321, 82 Stat. 164) is amended to read as follows:
TITLE IV--CREDIT REPAIR ORGANIZATIONS"
Sec.

SEC. 401. SHORT TITLE.(2)
This title may be cited as the 'Credit Repair Organizations Act'.

SEC. 402. FINDINGS AND PURPOSES.(3)
(a) Findings.--The Congress makes the following findings:
(1) Consumers have a vital interest in establishing and maintaining their credit worthiness and credit standing in order to obtain and use credit. As a result, consumers who have experienced credit problems may seek assistance from credit repair organizations which offer to improve the credit standing of such consumers.
(2) Certain advertising and business practices of some companies engaged in the business of credit repair services have worked a financial hardship upon consumers, particularly those of limited economic means and who are inexperienced in credit matters.
(b) Purposes.--The purposes of this title are--
(1) to ensure that prospective buyers of the services of credit repair organizations are provided with the information necessary to make an informed decision regarding the purchase of such services; and
(2) to protect the public from unfair or deceptive advertising and business practices by credit repair organizations.

SEC. 403. DEFINITIONS.(4)
For purposes of this title, the following definitions apply:
(1) Consumer. -- The term 'consumer' means an individual.
(2) Consumer credit transaction. -- The term 'consumer credit transaction' means any transaction in which credit is offered or extended to an individual for personal, family, or household purposes.
(3) Credit repair organization. -- The term 'credit repair organization'--
(A) means any person who uses any instrumentality of interstate commerce or the mails to sell, provide, or perform (or represent

that such person can or will sell, provide, or perform) any service, in return for the payment of money or other valuable consideration, for the express or implied purpose of--
(i) improving any consumer's credit record, credit history, or credit rating; or
(ii) providing advice or assistance to any consumer with regard to any activity or service described in clause (i); and
(B) does not include--
(i) any nonprofit organization which is exempt from taxation under section 501(c) (3) of the Internal Revenue Code of 1986;
(ii) any creditor (as defined in section 103 of the Truth in Lending Act),(5) with respect to any consumer, to the extent the creditor is assisting the consumer to restructure any debt owed by the consumer to the creditor; or
(iii) any depository institution (as that term is defined in section 3 of the Federal Deposit Insurance Act) or any Federal or State credit union (as those terms are defined in section 101 of the Federal Credit Union Act), or any affiliate or subsidiary of such a depository institution or credit union.
(4) Credit.--The term 'credit' has the meaning given to such term in section 103(e) of this Act.(6)

SEC. 404. PROHIBITED PRACTICES.(7) (a) In General.--No person may--
(1) make any statement, or counsel or advise any consumer to make any statement, which is untrue or misleading (or which, upon the exercise of reasonable care, should be known by the credit repair organization, officer, employee, agent, or other person to be untrue or misleading) with respect to any consumer's credit worthiness, credit standing, or credit capacity to-- (A) any consumer reporting agency (as defined in section 603(f) of this Act);(8) or (B) any person--
(i) who has extended credit to the consumer; or
(ii) to whom the consumer has applied or is applying for an extension of credit;

(2) make any statement, or counsel or advise any consumer to make any statement, the intended effect of which is to alter the consumer's identification to prevent the display of the consumer's credit record, history, or rating for the purpose of concealing adverse information that is accurate and not obsolete to--(A) any consumer reporting agency; (B) any person--
(i) who has extended credit to the consumer; or (ii) to whom the consumer has applied or is applying for an extension of credit;
(3) make or use any untrue or misleading representation of the services of the credit repair organization; or
(4) engage, directly or indirectly, in any act, practice, or course of business that constitutes or results in the commission of, or an attempt to commit, a fraud or deception on any person in connection with the offer or sale of the services of the credit repair organization.
(b) Payment in Advance.--No credit repair organization may charge or receive any money or other valuable consideration for the performance of any service which the credit repair organization has agreed to perform for any consumer before such service is fully performed.

SEC. 405. DISCLOSURES.(9)

(a) Disclosure Required.--Any credit repair organization shall provide any consumer with the following written statement before any contract or agreement between the consumer and the credit repair organization is executed:
'Consumer Credit File Rights Under State and Federal Law
You have a right to dispute inaccurate information in your credit report by contacting the credit bureau directly. However, neither you nor any "credit repair" company or credit repair organization has the right to have accurate, current, and verifiable information removed from your credit report. The credit bureau must remove accurate, negative information from your report only if it is over 7 years old. Bankruptcy information can be reported for 10 years. You have a right to obtain a copy of your credit report from

a credit bureau. You may be charged a reasonable fee. There is no fee, however, if you have been turned down for credit, employment, insurance, or a rental dwelling because of information in your credit report within the preceding 60 days. The credit bureau must provide someone to help you interpret the information in your credit file. You are entitled to receive a free copy of your credit report if you are unemployed and intend to apply for employment in the next 60 days, if you are a recipient of public welfare assistance, or if you have reason to believe that there is inaccurate information in your credit report due to fraud.

You have a right to sue a credit repair organization that violates the Credit Repair Organization Act. This law prohibits deceptive practices by credit repair organizations.
You have the right to cancel your contract with any credit repair organization for any reason within 3 business days from the date you signed it.

Credit bureaus are required to follow reasonable procedures to ensure that the information they report is accurate. However, mistakes may occur.

You may, on your own, notify a credit bureau in writing that you dispute the accuracy of information in your credit file. The credit bureau must then reinvestigate and modify or remove inaccurate or incomplete information. The credit bureau may not charge any fee for this service. Any pertinent information and copies of all documents you have concerning an error should be given to the credit bureau.

If the credit bureau's reinvestigation does not resolve the dispute to your satisfaction, you may send a brief statement to the credit bureau, to be kept in your file, explaining why you think the record is inaccurate. The credit bureau must include a summary of your statement about disputed information with any report it issues about you.

The Federal Trade Commission regulates credit bureaus and credit repair organizations. For more information contact:
The Public Reference Branch Federal Trade Commission Washington, D.C. 20580'.
(b) Separate Statement Requirement.--The written statement required under this section shall be provided as a document which is separate from any written contract or other agreement between the credit repair organization and the consumer or any other written material provided to the consumer.
(c) Retention of Compliance Records.--
(1) In general.--The credit repair organization shall maintain a copy of the statement signed by the consumer acknowledging receipt of the statement.
(2) Maintenance for 2 years.--The copy of any consumer's statement shall be maintained in the organization's files for 2 years after the date on which the statement is signed by the consumer.

SEC. 406. CREDIT REPAIR ORGANIZATIONS CONTRACTS.(10)
(a) Written Contracts Required.--No services may be provided by any credit repair organization for any consumer--
(1) unless a written and dated contract (for the purchase of such services) which meets the requirements of subsection
(b) has been signed by the consumer; or
(2) before the end of the 3-business-day period beginning on the date the contract is signed. (b) Terms and Conditions of Contract.--No contract referred to in subsection
(a) meets the requirements of this subsection unless such contract includes (in writing)--
(1) the terms and conditions of payment, including the total amount of all payments to be made by the consumer to the credit repair organization or to any other person;
(2) a full and detailed description of the services to be performed

by the credit repair organization for the consumer, including--
(A) all guarantees of performance; and
(B) an estimate of-- (i) the date by which the performance of the services (to be performed by the credit repair organization or any other person) will be complete; or (ii) the length of the period necessary to perform such services;
(3) the credit repair organization's name and principal business address; and
(4) a conspicuous statement in bold face type, in immediate proximity to the space reserved for the consumer's signature on the contract, which reads as follows: 'You may cancel this contract without penalty or obligation at any time before midnight of the 3rd business day after the date on which you signed the contract. See the attached notice of cancellation form for an explanation of this right.'.

SEC. 407. RIGHT TO CANCEL CONTRACT.(11)

(a) In General. -- Any consumer may cancel any contract with any credit repair organization without penalty or obligation by notifying the credit repair organization of the consumer's intention to do so at any time before midnight of the 3rd business day which begins after the date on which the contract or agreement between the consumer and the credit repair organization is executed or would, but for this subsection, become enforceable against the parties.

(b) Cancellation Form and Other Information. -- Each contract shall be accompanied by a form, in duplicate, which has the heading 'Notice of Cancellation' and contains in bold face type the following statement:
'You may cancel this contract, without any penalty or obligation, at any time before midnight of the 3rd day which begins after the date the contract is signed by you.
To cancel this contract, mail or deliver a signed, dated copy of this cancellation notice, or any other written notice to (name of credit repair organization) at (address of credit repair organization)

before midnight on (date)

I hereby cancel this transaction,

(date)

(purchaser's signature).'.

(c) Consumer Copy of Contract Required.--Any consumer who enters into any contract with any credit repair organization shall be given, by the organization--

(1) a copy of the completed contract and the disclosure statement required under section 405; and (2) a copy of any other document the credit repair organization requires the consumer to sign, at the time the contract or the other document is signed.

SEC. 408. NONCOMPLIANCE WITH THIS TITLE.(12)

(a) Consumer Waivers Invalid.--Any waiver by any consumer of any protection provided by or any right of the consumer under this title--

(1) shall be treated as void; and

(2) may not be enforced by any Federal or State court or any other person.

(b) Attempt To Obtain Waiver.--Any attempt by any person to obtain a waiver from any consumer of any protection provided by or any right of the consumer under this title shall be treated as a violation of this title.

(c) Contracts Not in Compliance.--Any contract for services which does not comply with the applicable provisions of this title--

(1) shall be treated as void; and

(2) may not be enforced by any Federal or State court or any other person.

SEC. 409. CIVIL LIABILITY.(13)

(a) Liability Established.--Any person who fails to comply with any provision of this title with respect to any other person shall be liable to such person in an amount equal to the sum of the amounts determined under each of the following paragraphs:

(1) Actual damages.--The greater of--

(A) the amount of any actual damage sustained by such person as a result of such failure; or

(B) any amount paid by the person to the credit repair organization.

(2) Punitive damages.--

(A) Individual actions.--In the case of any action by an individual, such additional amount as the court may allow.

(B) Class actions.--In the case of a class action, the sum of--

(i) the aggregate of the amount which the court may allow for each named plaintiff; and

(ii) the aggregate of the amount which the court may allow for each other class member, without regard to any minimum individual recovery.

(3) Attorneys' fees.--In the case of any successful action to enforce any liability under paragraph (1) or (2), the costs of the action, together with reasonable attorneys' fees.

(b) Factors to Be Considered in Awarding Punitive Damages.--In determining the amount of any liability of any credit repair organization under subsection (a)(2), the court shall consider, among other relevant factors--

(1) the frequency and persistence of noncompliance by the credit repair organization; (2) the nature of the noncompliance;

(3) the extent to which such noncompliance was intentional; and

(4) in the case of any class action, the number of consumers adversely affected.

SEC. 410. ADMINISTRATIVE ENFORCEMENT.(14)

(a) In General.--Compliance with the requirements imposed under this title with respect to credit repair organizations shall be enforced under the Federal Trade Commission Act by the Federal Trade Commission.

(b) Violations of This Title Treated as Violations of Federal Trade Commission Act.--

(1) In general. -- For the purpose of the exercise by the Federal

Trade Commission of the Commission's functions and powers under the Federal Trade Commission Act, any violation of any requirement or prohibition imposed under this title with respect to credit repair organizations shall constitute an unfair or deceptive act or practice in commerce in violation of section 5(a) of the Federal Trade Commission Act.

(2) Enforcement authority under other law. -- All functions and powers of the Federal Trade Commission under the Federal Trade Commission Act shall be available to the Commission to enforce compliance with this title by any person subject to enforcement by the Federal Trade Commission pursuant to this subsection, including the power to enforce the provisions of this title in the same manner as if the violation had been a violation of any Federal Trade Commission trade regulation rule, without regard to whether the credit repair organization--

(A) is engaged in commerce; or

(B) meets any other jurisdictional tests in the Federal Trade Commission Act. (c) State Action for Violations.--

(1) Authority of states. -- In addition to such other remedies as are provided under State law, whenever the chief law enforcement officer of a State, or an official or agency designated by a State, has reason to believe that any person has violated or is violating this title, the State--

(A) may bring an action to enjoin such violation;

(B) may bring an action on behalf of its residents to recover damages for which the person is liable to such residents under section 409 as a result of the violation; and

(C) in the case of any successful action under subparagraph (A) or (B), shall be awarded the costs of the action and reasonable attorney fees as determined by the court.

(2) Rights of commission.--

(A) Notice to commission.--The State shall serve prior written notice of any civil action under paragraph

(1) upon the Federal Trade Commission and provide the Commission with a copy of its complaint, except in any case

where such prior notice is not feasible, in which case the State shall serve such notice immediately upon instituting such action. (B) Intervention.--The Commission shall have the right-- (i) to intervene in any action referred to in subparagraph (A); (ii) upon so intervening, to be heard on all matters arising in the action; and (iii) to file petitions for appeal. (3) Investigatory powers. -- For purposes of bringing any action under this subsection, nothing in this subsection shall prevent the chief law enforcement officer, or an official or agency designated by a State, from exercising the powers conferred on the chief law enforcement officer or such official by the laws of such State to conduct investigations or to administer oaths or affirmations or to compel the attendance of witnesses or the production of documentary and other evidence. (4) Limitation. -- Whenever the Federal Trade Commission has instituted a civil action for violation of this title, no State may, during the pendency of such action, bring an action under this section against any defendant named in the complaint of the Commission for any violation of this title that is alleged in that complaint.

SEC. 411. STATUTE OF LIMITATIONS.(15)

Any action to enforce any liability under this title may be brought before the later of-- (1) the end of the 5-year period beginning on the date of the occurrence of the violation involved; or (2) in any case in which any credit repair organization has materially and willfully misrepresented any information which-- (A) the credit repair organization is required, by any provision of this title, to disclose to any consumer; and (B) is material to the establishment of the credit repair organization's liability to the consumer under this title, the end of the 5-year period beginning on the date of the discovery by the consumer of the misrepresentation.

SEC. 412. RELATION TO STATE LAW.(16)

This title shall not annul, alter, affect, or exempt any person subject to the provisions of this title from complying with any law of any State except to the extent that such law is inconsistent with any provision of this title, and then only to the extent of the inconsistency.

SEC. 413. EFFECTIVE DATE.(17)

This title shall apply after the end of the 6-month period beginning on the date of the enactment of the Credit Repair Organizations Act,(18) except with respect to contracts entered into by a credit repair organization before the end of such period.''.
1. Pub. L. No. 104-208, 110 Stat. 3009 (Sept. 30, 1996). The amendments to the credit statutes are in
Title II of the Act, entitled "Economic Growth and Regulatory Paperwork Reduction." The footnotes in this copy of the Act are not part of the Act, but are cross-references inserted by the FTC staff for the convenience of the reader.
2. To be codified as 15 U.S.C. § 1679. 3. To be codified as 15 U.S.C. § 1679a. 4. To be codified as 15 U.S.C. § 1679b.
5. Truth in Lending Act § 103(f) states in pertinent part: "The term 'creditor' refers only to creditros
who regularly extend, or arrange for the extension of, credit which is payable by agreement in more than four installments or for which the payment of a finance charge is or may be required, whether in connection with loans, sales pf property or services, or otherwise. . . ."
6. TILA § 103(e) states: "The term 'credit' means the right granted by a creditor to a debtor to defer payment of debt or to incur debt and defer its payment."
7. To be codified as 15 U.S.C. § 1679c.
8. Fair Credit Reporting Act (FCRA) § 603(f) states: "The term 'consumer reporting agency' means any person which, for monetary fees, dues, or on a cooperative nonprofit basis, regularly engages in whole or in part in the practice of assembling or evaluating consumer credit information or other information on consumers for the purpose of furnishing consumer reports to

third parties, and which uses any means or facility of interstate commerce for the purpose of preparing or furnishing consumer reports."

9. To be codified as 15 U.S.C. § 1679d. 10. To be codified as 15 U.S.C. § 1679e.

11. To be codified as 15 U.S.C. § 1679f.

12. To be codified as 15 U.S.C. § 1679g.

13. To be codified as 15 U.S.C. § 1679h.

14. To be codified as 15 U.S.C. § 1679i.

15. To be codified as 15 U.S.C. § 1679j.

16. To be codified as 15 U.S.C. § 1679k.

17. To be codified as 15 U.S.C. § 1679l.

18. The statute was signed by the President on September 30, 1996.

TABLE X

BONUS: THE 8 SECRET SCORES

1. **CREDIT-RISK SCORES:** These are the credit scores most of us know. The leading credit score, the FICO Score, was created by Fair Isaac and ranges from 300 – 850, with scores over 700 generally considered to be low risk.

2. **RESPONSE SCORE:** This score predicts the likelihood a consumer will respond to an offer of credit, such as a new card or a balance transfer offer. Credit card issuers use response scores to decide whom to target and how to customize offers to appeal to specific consumers.

3. **APPLICATION SCORE:** This score scoops up data from a consumer's credit application that's not included in their credit scores, including income, residential history or length of employment. Application scores are typically used in combination with other scores, to determine whether to open the account, what rate to give and how much credit to extend.

4. **BANKRUPTCY SCORE:** Credit scores typically predict the chance a consumer will miss a payment within the next 2 years. Bankruptcy scores predict the likelihood the consumer will file for Chapter 7 or a Chapter 13 repayment plan. Equifax produces the leading Bankruptcy Navigator Index or BNI credit scoring model. BNI's range from 1 to 300, with the higher the score, the lower the predicted risk.

5. **REVENUE SCORE:** Lenders want to maximize the profitability of each account, and one way they do that is to gauge how much money each account is likely to generate.

6. **ATTRITION-RISK SCORE:** Attrition risk refers to the likelihood a consumer will stop using a card, and attrition-risk scores are typically used in combination with other scores to determine what to do next if you look ready to bolt.

7. **TRANSACTION SCORE:** These are the scores that are run each time a consumer uses their plastic to determine whether the transaction should be approved. Issuers are typically looking for signs the transaction might be fraudulent, but transaction data can be used in other ways as well.

8. **COLLECTION SCORE:** The collection agencies use collection scores to assess the likelihood that that consumers will be able to pay them. These scores are used to sort their list of debtors by 'most likely' to pay to 'least likely' to pay. Collection agencies watch for all kinds of evidence that a consumer's financial status may be improving.

TABLE Y

56 DIFFERENT FICO SCORES

EXPERIAN (19)

FICO Risk Model V2 Auto

FICO Risk Model V2 Bankcard

FICO Risk Model V2 Generic

FICO Risk Model V2 Installment Loan

FICO Risk Model V2 Personal Finance

FICO Risk Model V3 Auto

FICO Risk Model V3 Bankcard

FICO Risk Model V3 Generic

FICO Risk Model V3 Installment Loan [1]

FICO Risk Model V3 Personal Finance

FICO Advanced Risk Score 1.0

FICO Advanced Risk Score 2.0

FICO Risk Model 08 Auto

FICO Risk Model 08 Bankcard

FICO Risk Model 08 Generic

FICO Risk Model 08 Mortgage

FICO Score 9

FICO Auto Score 9

FICO Bankcard Score 9

EQUIFAX (18)

Beacon 96 Auto

Beacon 96 Bankcard

Beacon 96 Generic

Beacon 96 Installment

Beacon 96 Personal Finance

Beacon 5.0 Auto

Beacon 5.0 Bankcard

Beacon 5.0 Generic

Beacon 5.0 Installment Loan

Beacon 5.0 Mortgage [1]

Beacon 5.0 Personal Finance

Pinnacle 1.0

Pinnacle 2.0

FICO Score 8

Beacon 09 Auto

Beacon 09 Bankcard

Beacon 09 Generic (Newest)

Beacon 09 Mortgage

TRANSUNION (19)

FICO Classic 98 Auto

FICO Classic 98 Bankcard

FICO Classic 98 Generic

FICO Classic 98 Installment

FICO Classic 98 Personal Finance

FICO NextGen

FICO Next Gen 03

FICO Classic 04 Auto

FICO Classic 04 Bankcard

FICO Classic 04 Generic

FICO Classic 04 Installment Loan [1]

FICO Classic 04 Personal Finance

FICO Classic 08 Auto

FICO Classic 08 Bankcard

FICO Classic 08 Generic

FICO Classic 08 Mortgage

FICO Score 9

FICO Auto Score 9

FICO Bankcard Score 9

---

[1] These Scoring Models are the most widely used by Mortgage Lenders as of 12/11/16

Aquarian Business Group, LLC

228 Park Ave S Suite 98477, New York, NY 10003

www.AquarianBusinessGroup.com

888.810.9590 opt. 1

ABOUT THE AUTHOR

Dominick Burke is a former loan officer with Aegis Lending, Guaranteed Home Mortgage and Consortium Financial. He is also Co-founder and Chief Financial Officer for Aquarian Business Group, LLC. He is FICO Pro Certified through AllRegs Academy. He is also FCRA/FACTA Certified through the Consumer Data Industry Association and has completed Cohort 4 Advanced Credit Training at the Credit Expert Summit. He is twice trained and qualified to be a Credit Expert Witness in State and Federal Court by John Ulzheimer, formerly of FICO and Experian. With over 16 years experience and over ten thousand satisfied 'creditworthy' consumers, Dominick has built a reputation that has attracted Celebrities and Professional Athletes that have had less-than-perfect credit. He currently conducts educational seminars about credit throughout the United States and has done seminars for Adrian O. Mapp (Mayor, Plainfield, NJ), Dana Williams (President, Passaic County New Jersey Board of Realtors), Michael Burke (State Commander of New York, VFW), Roy George (VP, Head of Compliance at Taylor Morrison Home Funding, Orlando, FL), Scott Tucker (District Manager at Coldwell Banker, Maryland) and Jenn Graziano (Creator, Producer Mob Wives Vh-1 series).

For Conference or Seminar Booking Requests
call: 1-888-810-9590 ext 925
To discuss any challenges with your credit call:
1-888-810-9590 option 1
Or email: crclient@aquarianbusinessgroup.com

www.ingramcontent.com/pod-product-compliance
Lightning Source LLC
Chambersburg PA
CBHW060445240326
41598CB00087B/3573